THE APPRENTICE

יהוה

THE APPRENTICE

THE WORLD AND THE UNIVERSE AS ONE

A
TREATISE
ON THE
FIRST DEGREE
OF
FREEMASONRY

by
A Brother of the Hermetic Art
∴ *Gregory* ∴ *B.* ∴ *Stewart* ∴

A.L. 6014

Other books by the author:
>   *What is Freemasonry, ebook (online)*
>   *Masonic Traveler – Essays and Commentary (print)*
>   *Masonic Traveler, FreemasonInformation.com (online)*

Coming Soon:
>   *Fellow of the Craft (2015)*
>   *Master Mason (2015)*

THE APPRENTICE
The World and the Universe As One
A Treatise on the First Degree of Freemasonry

by Gregory B. Stewart

Copyright ©2014, FmI Publishing
ISBN 978-0-9862041-0-4
Library of Congress PCN 2014921224

First Printing

Published by FmI Publishing
P.O. Box 14204
Los Angeles, CA 91409

www.FreemasonInformation.com
email: masonictraveler@gmail.com

Questions, comments, inquiries – please send correspondence to the email or address above.

Art, Text and Design by
Gregory Stewart, 2011–2014

*Dedicated
to
Those in Pursuit
of the
Hermetic Art*

∴ L ∴ V ∴ X ∴

Thank you to the following people who without their support this book would not have been published:

Gord Echlin, Davide Riboli, Joseph James, Jorge Dagang, Jeffrey S. Kupperman, Carlos A. Rodriguez, Saint Cloud Lodge #221; Ann Arbor-Fraternity Lodge No. 262, F. & A.M., Michigan; John R. Merrick, Daniel Barston, Kelly Feldcamp, Randy Reese, Seth Allen, Nicholas Vettese, Jeff Ewing, John D. Spreckels Lodge #657; June E. Lennon, Freemason; Bro. Alex Towey, Johnny Arias, Gar Pickering, Chris Cochrane, Melissa Howe-Pomeranz, Gary Iverson, Luis A. Feliciano, Stewart A. Anderson, Andrew Smith, Kirk Bielskis, mmg86, Prenna Sergent, Matt Frye, Corey Hilton, Jason Hawkinson-Prater, Thomas Butler, J. A. Foster, Christopher Davis, Dominic J. Tufo, F.&A.M., California; David W. Douglas, Ireland, Shanan Hough, Shawn Michaels and Philip Michael Hugh Lawson

For D.S.

my

everything...

ILLUSTRATIONS

I. The Allegorical Tree (fronts piece), pen and ink, 2014*

II. Societas Sub Rosa (inside fronts piece), pen and ink, 2013*

III. Ordo Structor, (title page) Masons Mark, digital, 2006*

IV. Ein Sof into Malkuth, pen and ink, 2014*

V. The Tree of Life, ink wash on paper, 2014*

VI. The Sacrifice of Mithras, artists of Pergamon, 200AD

VII. Il Monte Santo Di Dio, print, Baccio Baldini, 1477

Illustrated by the author

CONTENTS

Preface	XI
The Ein Sof	XXIV
Creation	XXVI
The Apprentice	35
Spiritual Initiation	77
Order from Chaos	83
Notes	91
Footnotes	95
Index	101

PREFACE

Force, Unregulated...

This work you have in your hand is the product of many years of consideration and study. While it may invoke certain truths, the symbolic aspects of its consideration, like all things in the material universe, are fluid. The degrees of the Scottish Rite are an amalgamation of rites and ceremonies assembled over centuries, composed, deconstructed and then recomposed again and again in a cycle of maturation, death and rebirth. As the modern Rite has evolved, so too has the arrangement and usage of the degrees evolved. This work is an attempt to collect in a textual snapshot the author's understanding of the First

Degree of Scottish Rite Freemasonry.

One note important to impart is that the work of early Scottish Rite Freemasonry conveyed and inspired future fraternal societies and the operations of other esoteric and occultic thinkers. While it would be impossible to say whether there is a direct connection to the esoteric workings of these quasi-mystical and magical groups, at the deepest levels of their ethos, the ideas and words rendered by Pike in *Morals and Dogma* resonates within them. It strikes me that some authors and teachers sensed the depth of Pike's ideas when they created their own quasi-Masonic programs of initiation. Programs such as the Golden Dawn, Builders of the Adytum and even more remote outliers such as AMORC and the OTO. While each has its own unique tradition, they share themes, notes and tones of what the early Scottish Rite proposed. Like genetic brothers, they evolved from a common source, part of which being *Morals and Dogma*.

Rather than try and approach this from an

PREFACE

academic stand point of deconstructing lineages and connections, what better way to understand the symbolic and allegorical meanings than by deconstructing the symbolic path to finding its parallels and deeper meanings? An oft-heard lament in Temples is a lack of contemporary understanding of the allegorical allusions from the past. Greek and Latin no longer the in vernacular of the education system; Shakespearean prose replaced with bite-sized *"infotainment"* without the faintest trace of moral and ethical ideations. It is no wonder the allegorical lessons of Freemasonry are becoming lost in the noise of the Modern Age. If that is the case, then, the ideas of the Scottish Rite were lost long ago.

This work, while rude and rough, is an instrument to constraining what remains of that force of a productive and regulated effort. Pike, in opening his *Morals and Dogma*, writes:

"FORCE, unregulated or ill-regulated, is not only wasted in the void, like that of gunpowder burned in the open air, and steam unconfined by science; but,

 THE APPRENTICE

striking in the dark...its blows meeting only the air, they recoil and bruise itself. It is destruction and ruin. It is the volcano, the earthquake, the cyclone;--not growth and progress."

Let this stand as an attempt at ameliorating that destruction so as to preserve once again growth and progress.

Greg Stewart
Los Angeles, California
Autumn, A.L. 6014

PREFACE

FREEMASONRY DEFINED

An explanation for those new to the fraternity

Freemasonry is a post-collegiate male fraternity dedicated to the spiritual development of the initiate into a broader sense of the self, how he relates to the Divine, and his contributory role in the world. It conveys this message through a series of progressive degrees initiating the candidate into a deeper level of understanding and membership. Ultimately, the raised Master Mason is given the allegorical tools to further work on and develop his Masonic intuition.

The largest and oldest fraternal order in the world, Freemasonry crosses all religious boundaries to bring together its adherents of all countries, sects, and opinion in peace and harmony to work towards the betterment of all mankind.

THE APPRENTICE

A universal brotherhood, Freemasonry is dedicated to serving the divine through service to family, country, and humankind.

Freemasonry is a philosophical organization emphasizing the study of moral symbols to build character in its participants. This education is, in part, the foundation of a more profound understanding of mankind and his existence in society.

SCOTTISH RITE FREEMASONRY

The college of Freemasonry, the Scottish Rite presents the advanced degrees of Freemasonry beyond that of the third degree or Master Mason. Scottish Rite Freemasonry degrees are further education on the principals of the Craft Lodge with their own perspective of the three principal degrees in the lodge of perfection.

Scottish Rite Freemasonry is a compelling

PREFACE

and conquering spiritual force, the reasons of which are revealed in the degrees.

A common definition of the society says, "Scottish Freemasonry is the foe of intolerance, fanaticism, and superstition. It battles every form of racial and sectarian prejudice and bigotry. It is a mighty exponent of freedom in thought, religion, and government. Thus, the Scottish Rite is a rite of instruction. It interprets the symbols and allegories of Masonry in the light of history and philosophy using the words of the supreme prophets of humanity, ceremonies of the great religions of the world, and significant episodes from history to point the moral and adorn the tale."

 THE APPRENTICE

DOUBLEHEAD EAGLE

Mackey in his *Encyclopedia of Freemasonry*, quoting from the transactions of *Quatuor Coronati Lodge*, pages 214, volume xxiv, 1911, says of the adoption of the Scottish Rite usage:

"The most ornamental, not to say the most ostentatious feature of the insignia of the Supreme Council, 33 , of the Ancient and Accepted (Scottish) Rite, is the double-headed eagle, surmounted by an imperial crown. This device seems to have been adopted some time after 1755 by the grade known as the Emperors of the East and West; a sufficiently pretentious title. This seems to have been its first appearance in connection with Freemasonry, but history of the high grades has been subjected to such distortion that it is difficult to accept unreservedly any assertion put forward regarding them. From this imperial grade, the double-headed eagle

 PREFACE

came to the 'Sovereign Prince Masons' of the Rite of Perfection. The Rite of Perfection with its 25 Degrees was amplified in 1801, at Charleston, United States of America, into the Ancient and Accepted Rite of 33, with the double-headed eagle for its most distinctive emblem. When this emblem was first adopted by the high grades it had been in use as a symbol of power for 5000 years, or so. No heraldic bearing, no emblematic device anywhere today can boast such antiquity. It was in use a thousand years before the Exodus from Egypt, and more than 2000 years before the building of King Solomon's Temple."

 THE APPRENTICE

LODGE of PERFECTION

The Symbolic Lodge and the Ineffable Degrees

The first portion of the Scottish Rite system of degrees is dubbed *The Lodge of Perfection*. This series of degrees includes the 1° through the 14° and are referred to as the ineffable degrees, taken from the Latin *ineffibilis* meaning something that should not be spoken (incapable of being expressed or described in words; inexpressible. Not to be spoken because of its sacredness; unutterable).

PREFACE

APPRENTICE

From the Old French *aprentiz* "someone learning" (c.1300, Modern French *apprenti*, taking the older form as a plural), "unskilled, inexperienced," from *aprendre* (Modern French *apprendre*) "to learn; to teach," contracted from Latin *apprehendere* (see apprehend).

Online Etymology Dictionary

apprehend - mid-14c., "to grasp in the senses or mind," from Old French aprendre (12c.)

apprehensible - capable of being understood.

The teachings of these readings are not
sacramental, so far as they go beyond
the realm of morality into those
of other domains of
Thought and
Truth

 THE APPRENTICE

THE EIN SOF

Chaos gives birth to order
    from the swirling nothing of the infinite.

The idea of the creator brings forth dimension.

Flat and round like a single cell of life
    the cosmic everything begins.

Within this wide vast creation
    a tree begins to root.

One of many, it is unique of species and genius
    from its trunk
        within its limbs
            to the tips of its furthest reaches.

Each turn of the knot
    growth of bark
        vein of leaf
            and drop of sap
                serving to enlighten us
                    as to our being.

PREFACE

Our connection begins in the manner of the seed
    blown, carried, transported
        through the microcosmed universe.
Its life, beginning at the moment of its infinite journey in
    the aether
        ending with its impregnation into the
        firmament.
The proof of its creation and growth
    in its crowned canopy
        composed of natural elemental strength
    in its survival
        ecstatic celestial beauty
        in its adornment
        and cosmic wisdom
            from its time observing
            its domain.

    Its arboreal existence,
        truly,

        ...was a Tree of Life.

 THE APPRENTICE

CREATION

Composed of difference, opposites, and imbalance
*   betwixt life and death*
*   oblivion and infinity*

The elements essence of earth, fire, water and spirit
*   coalesce into consciousness.*

Decision is action, the spark of intuitive realization
*   of that invisible force beyond the veil of vision.*

Out from the Chaos of the infinite
*   the Ein Sof of nothingness*
*   gives birth to the seed of Malkuth.*

The germ of all that is...
*   has been...*
*   ...ever shall be.*

From its manifestation will bloom
*   ...strength*
*   ...beauty*
*   ...and wisdom*

Of different compositions
*   but as the same composite source.*

PREFACE

Every man and every woman is a star.
*   the seeds from which our existence roars*
*   to life anew.*

Blooming into a crowning canopy under
the star decked heavens
*   the earthly composition of alchemical*
*   transformation.*
*   The dross becoming meaningful.*
*   The mundane, majestic.*

This is our gate to the infinite above
*   as our spirit takes shape below*
*   the beginning, the earth*

The stars of the divine in the great beyond
*   in the imagination of our creation.*

Thus thy body, O Child of earth and sky,
Is truly the Heavenly Vision of the
Goodness of the Eternal.
This thy body is the Palace of the King;
This thy body is the manifested world
of God and man;
This thy body is the seamless robe of ADONAI
For I am thy Lord
And the Lord and His Temple are ONE

PAUL FOSTER CASE
EPILOGOS, THE MEDITATION ON MALKUTH
THE BOOK OF TOKENS

...how awesome is this place!
This is none other than the house of God;
this is the gate of
Heaven.

Genesis 28:17
(NIV)

THE APPRENTICE

 THE APPRENTICE

EIN SOF (OR AYN SOF) INTO MALKUTH
THE ENDLESS ONE, NO END, UNENDING, BECOMING
GREG STEWART, PEN & INK ON BOARD, 2014

THE
APPRENTICE

*Let your mind seek for light, truth and liberty
in this new world, and they will surely
come to you.*

FIRST DEGREE, SCOTTISH RITE BLUE LODGE

To say there is a first degree of Scottish Rite masonry may come as a surprise. As most commonly practiced, the Scottish Rite is a system of quasi-religious allegorical morality plays divided into degrees that begin in progression following the traditional three-degree system of Masonic initiation in the most prevalent practice of blue, or craft, lodge Freemasonry today. As they are laid out, the Scottish Rite craft lodge degrees run in parallel with the first three degrees of the Webb Preston York Rite System of Freemasonry, which is the dominant system of the Masonic lodge ritual adopted in American Grand Lodge

 THE APPRENTICE

Masonry in the early 1800s. The Scottish Rite degrees, however, began in an earlier era, which leads seamlessly into what we know of today as the 4th through 32nd Scottish Rite system. Only a few lodges still practice the Scottish Rite's precursor degrees, most notably the blue lodge in the state of Louisiana, as the degrees are said to retain much of their earlier European and French roots.[1] Much of what is contained in those degrees mirrors what is common practice in the York degrees, but there are differences and it is in those aspects of divergence that these earlier rituals hold some parlance for the Scottish Rite. In their totality, they retain the elements familiar to any who have undergone their practice in other traditions with a greater degree of symbolism and esoteric emphasis. To see this, we must look to the earlier rituals so that we can find their fundamentals of esoteric scholarship which are the roots taught in the Rite as elucidated by Albert Pike and promulgated in the present-day system. These differences in the degrees become especially obvious in his analysis found in *Morals and Dogma*, giving us the opportunity to look at why and what those differences suggest. For those readers who are not Scottish Rite masons, the degrees, and the lessons taught in the multitude of Scottish Rite Valleys across America today suggest a link between the Scottish Rite teachings by degree and the teachings of mystical Kabbalah, more precisely as teachings spread upon the Kabbalistic Tree of Life, something brought to the attention of the Scottish Rite candidates in the lecture of the fourth degree. In the fourth degree, the connection to the Kabbalah and the Tree of Life is made loosely without significant parallels or representation of how, or why, the two hold parallels. But, in close analysis of the progressive degrees, it becomes very clear to say that there is a distinct connection between the 32 degrees, the 10 Sephirot and the 22 paths that compose a universal representation of the esoteric Tree. As the fourth degree mention of the

Rite's connection to the Kabbalah is only a superficial reference, it is our starting point to see the two as related, necessitating a more extensive exploration of the following degrees within which we can find a multitude of parallels in the Rites' symbolic operation and construction. As one begins to climb the allegorical Tree through the degree, it becomes obvious very quickly that veiled in its canopy are metaphorical links, ineffable symbols, and outright allegorical references to the connections between them - something that many writers (both Masonic and lay) have suggested, through a variety of esoteric systems of study. Was Pike's system intended to mirror an ancient Jewish system of esoteric theology, or a device made use of by Pike to capture with such detail the similarities that he saw between them? As you will begin to see, it is the latter as the degrees lack the theology of Judaism, instead taking on their parallel structure while borrowing from this older tradition in a way that he constructs a natural compliment of

THE WORLD AND THE UNIVERSE AS ONE

one to another, such that the two have become so intricately linked - the Kabbalah of old intermingled with the Christian Mysticism of the Cabala of the new becoming a syncretic blend of spiritual Qabalah unencumbered by strict religious dogma. Throughout his work, Pike keeps the systems separate acknowledging the notion of a singular God placing the system into a predominately religious worldview though unlikely recognizable to the broader Christian community today. With the skill of a master artisan, Pike weaves a tapestry of old and new thoughts together, knitting the details of what he sees as the ideas that underlie all modern religions tying back into the system that is the inheritor of those combined faiths into a unifying rite or uniform religious practice. That choice to link the degrees of Freemasonry, an old system at the time of Pike's own contributions, to those ideas of even older esoteric teaching, revived as best he could the connections to a Hermetic tradition that has given root to several modern magi-

THE APPRENTICE

cal offshoot systems today.[2] But, before the work of those traditions could build on Pike's, they needed to be welded together into an amalgam of ideas that transcended the oblique esoterica of their diverse histories such that they have become inseparable from the deeper meaning of the degrees from which they grew out of. While Masonry may not delve into magical practice, incantations or angelic evocation, at its root is a process of transformation through ritual and allegorical symbolism meant to convey a spiritual growth within the student of its mysteries. The lessons, with their Qabalistic teachings, have interlaced in a way that to change their composition would change the very fabric of the Scottish Rite itself. To that end the degrees, both the lower three and the higher 30, are in and of themselves a complete system which forms a circuit of learning which is its own birth, baptism, and maturation, that climbs ever higher into the allegorical Tree of Life towards the pinnacle of its branches high a top the canopy at

THE WORLD AND THE UNIVERSE AS ONE

the completion of the 32nd degree where, it is hoped, one will find an understanding of the self and one's place within the allegorical universe. But, before we reach that philosophical apex, we must first start at the beginning, or perhaps the starting place of the beginning at the very roots of the symbolic Tree of Life, at the point just before the degree system unfolds where we can begin to construct our understanding. That starting point is outside the temple in the space before the door of the lodge room as the aspirant for the degrees makes his first fateful knock, which is the essence of what the first degree represents. To enter that space we must start with an explanation of the Kabbalah and our entry point through the degrees of Masonry into the Tree of Life from the chaos of the *Ein Sof* and into the Sephirot of *Malkuth*.

Before we can begin to understand the relationship between the system of Scottish Rite Masonry and our study of the Kabbalah, we must first grasp what is meant in its study as

relative to the system of Freemasonry. The Kabbalah, in its traditional consideration, is a discipline based upon a school of thought and religious teaching that is concerned with the mystical aspect of Rabbinic Judaism, the study of which can be traced to the 11th century when a full theological system emerged from the text of the *Sepher Yetzirah*, whose antecedents are linked to as early as the 2nd century CE, and whose surviving commentaries resurfaced in the 10th century.[3] Of particular note to Scottish Rite Masonry is a passage of the *Sepher Yetzirah* which describes how the universe was created by the *"God of Israel"* through *"32 wondrous ways of wisdom"*[4] - an idea that seems to have resonated with Pike in his adoption and reassembly of the Scottish Rite degrees in parallel with the Tree of Life.

The over-arching goal of the study of the Kabbalah/Cabala is that through its study, the student seeks to define the nature of the universe and the human being, their spiritual and

THE WORLD AND THE UNIVERSE AS ONE

earthly relationship and the nature and purpose of existence. Additionally, it presents methods to aid understanding of these concepts, and symbolic correlations, which facilitates the student's aspirational study to thereby attain a degree of spiritual realization - a process much in line with the study and practice of Freemasonry. In traditional Judaism, the system of Kabbalah draws extensively on the rich history of thought using its source of Jewish teaching to explain and demonstrate its esoteric ideas. These teachings began to spread into Europe with the expulsion of the Jews from Spain circulating in a time of renewed discovery of Greek and Roman writings which re-entered Europe and were embraced by a Christian sub-current that found resonance with the philosophies using Mysticism as a means to understand the faith through a re-discovered Hermetic lens. This study in Western Europe can be attributed to the work of the Italian Giovanni Pico della Mirandola who was one of the first to translate the Kab-

THE APPRENTICE

balah in 1484. His translation for the Medici Court began to circulate and receive wider study along with other works, including the *Corpus Hermeticium*, which were the collected works believed attributed to Hermes Trismegistus. It was in these developments that the foundation was laid for the Kabbalah to be studied by a wider ecclesial underground.[5] In time, this study of the Kabbalah/Cabala evolved and was adopted into more current Hermetic practice, quite likely as an outgrowth of Pike's work in the Scottish Rite, which is today a present-day practice of the Hermetic system of Kabbalah. This third form of study, commonly expressed as *Qabalah*, deals more extensively with ideas of what we would consider today to be *New Age* (or new thought) thinking, including elements of the tarot, astrology, Neo-Platonism, Gnosticism, Hermetism and Hermeticism, striking a parlance with traditions that include Rosicrucianism, Enocian and Solomnic angelic magick systems and other similar esoteric confluences up to and including neo-paganism. It is very important to say that *Hermetic Qabalah* differs from the strict Jewish form of *Kabbalah* or the Christian mysticism of *Cabala* in that it includes a wider degree of syncretism - a fact that readers can tease from a close reading of Pike's *Morals and Dogma* and examination of its inclusion of different theologies.

It is in this study, however, that many of the ideas, symbols, and concepts from the Christian Cabala factor into the overt study of the Tree of Life, which is the seeming foundation that Pike used as the basis of the 32 Scottish Rite degrees.

So how does that pertain to our exploration? At the beginning of our study, and the practice of Masonry, aspirants are oriented into a unique position of observation, thrust into a vast matrix of progressive degrees to facilitate a particular spiritual/ethical development. The students of this tradition are, in the process of their initiation, taken into an archetypal world which goes beyond the physical and into the metaphorical

 THE APPRENTICE

universe. In it, they imaginatively exist amid a collection of elements that swirl and move about around them. At some point, amid that chaos, an elemental consciousness awakens in the neophyte to their broader existence and the invisible forces at work around them. It is that awakening that becomes the impetus to bring the aspirant into contact with the fraternity.

The World and the Universe as One

Following their consideration and application of the mystical traditions, they inspire to rise above the swirling chaos of the universe around them and come into association with the fraternity. In short, this process describes the coalescence of order out of the chaos, which is the journey of Ein Sof into the Sephiroth of Malkuth, which *is* the initiation into the first degree.

Composed of the four worldly elements (earth, water, fire, and air) Malkuth's gross representation may on the surface appear to represent the physical world. Yet, like all allegorical figures, we find there to be a deeper correspondence between those elements and their greater meaning. By extension, the four elemental worlds within the sphere of Malkuth are representations of our existence as having both a physical form and a spiritual idea which, together, form a *Prima Materia*[6], the ideal of the world itself as the four spiritual elements. This idea of a *Prima Matera* has resonance to the alchemical process of separation and union, as it is

 THE APPRENTICE

from a chaotic combination of elements that the alchemist seeks to separate and re-form a substance into a singular elemental form. We catch a glimpse of this in the work of the Swiss alchemist Paracelsus, whose use of the word *'chaos'* is synonymous with *'element'* as a primeval chaos that is imagined as a formless congestion of all elements. Heinrich Khunrath, in the alchemical treatise *Chaos* (1597), quotes Paracelsus on the point saying that *"The light of the soul, by the will of the Triune God, made all earthly things appear from the primal Chaos.*[7]*"* Israel Regardie, the compiler of the Golden Dawn, takes the idea of *Prima Matera*, or primal chaos, and links it to the *'Shekhinah'* which he defines as the *"spiritual presence of Ain Soph as a heritage of mankind and an ever present reminder of spiritual verities."*[8]

To understand this, one must first conceive what the Ein Sof (alternatively written Ain Sof/Ain Soph) represents in the system of the Kabbalah. From the *Zohar*, the formless creative universe, the *Prima Materia*, is considered as the causeless cause of all manifestation, which is the essence of Ein Sof, and essentially, the creative power (or idea) at the creation behind the force that created creation itself, the God before God. It is this power at work that results in the coalescence of Malkuth as the aspirant for the degrees enters into the courtyard of the Freemasonry.

Pike captures this idea as he opens his commentary in *Morals and Dogma* by defining that force as a power that is *"unregulated or ill regulated ... like that of gun powder burned in the open air."* With this analogy, Pike tries to capture the idea of the creative force of the creator, the Ein Sof into Malkuth, relating it to the activity of the aspirant before he knocks at the temple door - essentially in the process of the aspirant in deciding to undertake his initiation in the degrees. Pike continues on this construct of force, suggesting that it must have *"a brain and a law such that its deeds of daring produce permanent results"* where *"there is real progress"* giving the force reason for its transformation in the first place. It is

here, in Pike's example of the gunpowder, that we can see the purpose of the transformation, which is to subsequently undergo its own transformation. Rather than the unfocused explosive force, erupting ineffectually into the universe at its ignition, the force is directed and channeled for a higher purpose, its energy being the product of its effort that is the conductor to further progress and change. So to is the operation of transformation from Ein Sof into Malkuth, and the entry point of Masonry.

An important point that needs to be made clear is to mention that in most Western esoteric systems of study - including Mystery School Qabalah traditions, the Tree of Life is traversed from a top-down approach in which the student moves from the crown of Kether, at the top, to our point here in Malkuth, at the bottom. As this degree introduces us to the Scottish Rite schema, as devised and committed to study by Pike, it suggests that it takes a reverse approach to the traditional, perhaps more rational, pro-

The World and the Universe as One

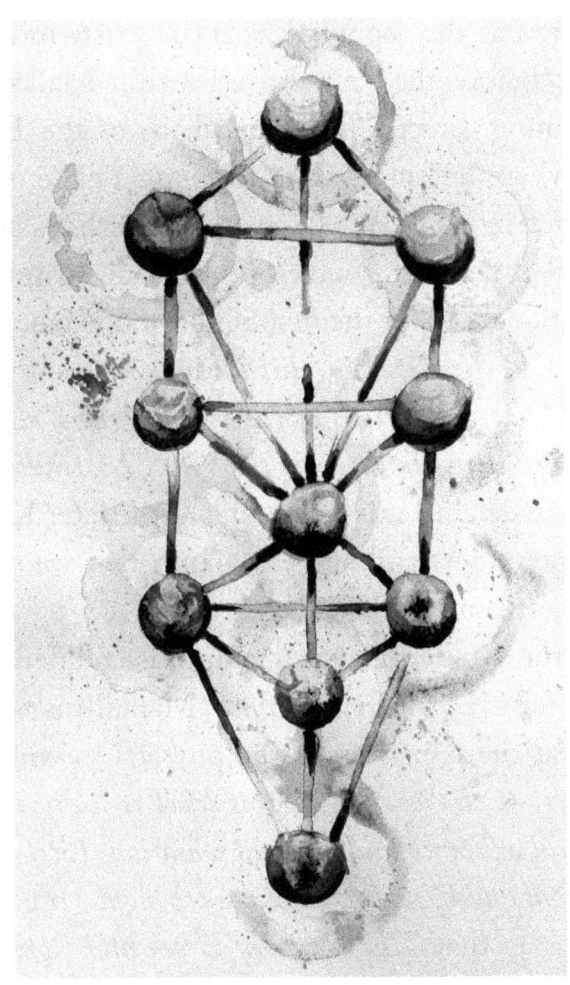

THE TREE OF LIFE

gression as the aspirant/candidate exists in the space before the first degree within Malkuth, stemming directly from the chaos of the Ein Sof where he enters from the roots of the tree. Kircher, in his *Oedipus Aegyptiacus* (perhaps one of Pike's earliest sources of Kabbalistic interpretations) says of the first Sephirot of Malkuth that it is the *"Assisting Intelligence because it directs all the operations of the seven planets, with their divisions, and concurs their in."*[9] An interesting parallel, but it is in looking at the later Kabbalistic understanding of Malkuth that we can take some interesting steps.

In the Golden Dawn working, as codified in Crowley's *Argenteum Astrum*[10], Malkuth is considered the Kingdom of the physical to which it says, *"Consciousness at this level is limited to physical existence and physical sensation. Little occurs that could be called self aware thought."* It goes on to say that *"The Hades of Greek and Roman legend is the lowest level of existence, the level of spiritless, soulless shells. Malkuth is Hades unless it is joined to higher states of consciousness."* In using both the Kircher system and the much later Golden Dawn/Crowley tradition, we can, perhaps, validate our approach through the Rite as a Qaballistic system from Malkuth then moving upwards. This is a subject that will begin to take shape as we ascend further in our study of the degrees from the unique Scottish Rite perspective.

In the operation of the first degree ritual, as found in the workings of the Scottish Rite Blue Lodge degree,[11] we find parity with this esoteric progression as the candidate is introduced into the lodge upon the *"torture of his flesh"* and instructed that the condition upon which he enters is to "*impress upon [his] mind the circumstances attending the introduction of man upon earth, his entrance to a new and untried existence with a world to conquer and subdue."* It continues to read that as he enters into this new world state of being, he is *"blind and helpless"* from a place where "chaos reins supreme." His goal, as it is for

 THE APPRENTICE

all those who have undertaken similar steps, is to seek light.

At its simplest terms, this entry describes the coalescence of energy, the four elements in both physical terms and in their spiritual interpretation seeking what will, presently, become that luminous destination which is alluded to. Looking to the degree, it spells out what the candidate personifies - that he is *"the primal state of man after his creation, our darkness of being without knowledge or focus"*- or unregulated force. This could perhaps be construed as the moment of Adam's creation in the Judeo/Christian tradition which tells us in *Genesis 1:26 "Then God said, 'Let us make mankind in our image, in our likeness, so that they may rule over the fish in the sea and the birds in the sky, over the livestock and all the wild animals, and over all the creatures that move along the ground.'"* Like this verse in which Adam is immediately given dominion of the world he was created into so too, in very rapid form, the candidate is taken from this rude, chaotic state and made into a focused expression of elemental energy, a state of both motion and stillness, something that Dion Fortune points to as an attribute of the Sephiroth Malkuth.

Fortune, in her Qaballistic opus *The Mystical Qabalah*, points to the inertia of Malkuth as the source where the Sephirot's virtue resides.[12] To look back at the state of the creator's creation, the degree, and the Sephirot, in a symbolic sense, becomes the created world and the universe as a singular interwoven emanation. As the traditional study of Kabbalah suggests the precursor state of being, Ein Sof, is an invisible or limitless Sephirot defined as God prior to his self manifestation - the divine origin translated as the unending or without end. In similar form, man was without expression until the point that the Great Architect imagined him into being; that point of Adam's creation in Genesis. So too is the First Degree entered into as such, the point before entry where other realities are possible and the point immediately following our becoming an 'entered' apprentice where those who undertake the ritual are solidified upon the path of being. We can associate this process as represented in the passage over the tessellated border of the checkered floor - visually, the movement in space from the formless exterior to inside the geometric sphere of creation. This may seem a radical step, but as the degree is the entry point of the Masonic system, in its creation is the need of a beginning, the beginning before the beginning, and that is what this first Sephirot Malkuth represents.

Here we reach a parallel of Malkuth and the first degree of Scottish Rite Masonry in which the Sephirot finds resonance with an attribution made by both Dion Fortune and later Israel Rigiardie wherein Malkuth is called *"the Gate"* - quite literally we are entering through a gate onto this path to begin its instruction. Upon entry the candidate is given a lesson of virtue and vice which is to illustrate the process in our decision-making between good and bad decisions and their resulting outcomes. These lessons become the framework of our advancement, but not before the candidate is ushered through that "gate" and taken upon a journey representing the creative elemental state he has just coalesced out of. The stages of that journey are delineated as earth, water, and fire - each with its own unique lessons to impart.

Earth, in the degree, is said to be the entrance of the candidate into a new world of thought as he is *"left to grope his way amid the darkness of the first night"* where his senses are *"oppressed and overwhelmed"* which is *"intended to inculcate the weakness of man - when alone and unassisted by light."* The goal of this journey is to *"...give us a glimpse of undiscovered fields"* to *"show man his own weakness, and bring him to a more patient and respectful consideration of the claims due his fellow-beings."*[13]

Next, the candidate undergoes a journey of water which is said to teach that the *"predominating principal within him is determined by his*

 THE APPRENTICE

own will and choice," good choices leading to cheerful contentment and bad choices to a *"bitter remorse."* Interestingly, the degree instructor then says that water is an instrument for effecting change, be it the rough shaping of mountains or the chaotic action of the surging seas, but also in a subtle manner with the atmosphere of renewing energy to animal and vegetable life - even restoring man to purity both as maker and himself, through a tear of repentance.

Having completed the voyages of earth and water, the candidate is taken next upon a trial by fire. The connection here draws its parallel from the ancient mysteries and the separation of elements (earth and liquid water) into their pure components through the operation of fire. This gives us an interesting aspect of alchemy to explore as it is through fire that we are thought to be transformed. In this portion of the lecture, it reads that the *"fire burning in man's heart 'will' rise like the fabled Phoenix pure from ashes of corruption."* As in the alchemical process, the transformation necessary to reach the completion is our consumption by flame so as to reach a point where we can rise above our base self.

Passing these stages, the candidate is in a position to undertake his next elemental trial, but one different from the others. Unlike the preceding three elemental trials, the fourth trial of what should be air is more aptly understood as a trial of *spirit* as the candidate of the ritual is now made to give his obligation into the degree making him an Apprentice to the craft. This trial of spirit begins with the candidate taking a draught of bitters so as to teach him that even the most joyous laughter will be turned to bitter tears, preparing him to withstand disappointment in *"what ever form it appears."*

From hereon the degree resembles its York Rite practice with only a few points of deviation, such as an acknowledgment of the head of John the Baptist as a symbol of Honor, Justice, and Virtue. Surprisingly absent in the Scottish Rite degree work is the symbol of Jacob's ladder,

 The Apprentice

at least in so much as in the physical work of the degree to make the aspirant/candidate into a Mason. Pike however, in his treatise in *Morals and Dogma*, delves into the allegorical symbolism of the ladder to explore the vestiges of its meaning in other mystery/religious traditions that he sees as woven into this Masonic tradition. In his writings, Pike notes the ladder as coming from an older tradition, likely from the Mithraic Mystery traditions of antiquity.

As a mystery cult tradition, the Mithraic Mysteries were practiced early in the Roman Empire sometime between the 1st and 4th centuries AD. It is thought that worshippers of Mithras developed a complex system of initiation believed to be based upon seven grades in parallel with astrology and its associated planets. In its most common practice the Mithraic traditions are understood to consist of ritual meals and ceremonies, but little else is known of their exact nature. In the *Suda*, a 10th century Byzantine encyclopedia of the ancient Mediterra-

The World and the Universe as One

An Illustration of THE SACRIFICE OF MITHRAS, circa 200 A.D.
A typical representation of Mithra, originally in white marble now in the Louvre Paris, taken from the Mithrseum of the Capitol.

From Franz Valery Marie Cumont's The Mysteries of Mithra:

"Mithra is sacrificing the bull in the cave The characteristic features of the Mithra monuments are all represented here the youths with the upright and the inverted torch the snake the dog the raven Helios the god of the sun and Selene the goddess of the moon Owing to the Phrygian cap the resemblance of the face to that of Alexander and the imitation of the motif of the classical Greek group of Nike sacrificing a bull all characteristics of the Diadochian epoch the original of all the works of this type has been attributed to an artist of Pergamon."

nean world, it says of Mithrism that *"no one was permitted to be initiated into them (the mysteries of Mithras), until he should show himself holy and steadfast by undergoing several graduated tests"*[15] which gives us a glimpse of its operational links to masonry. Initiates in this practice called themselves syndexioi, those who were *"united by the handshake"* which is suggested to represent the shaking of hands between the demi-god Mithras and Sol, the solar representation of deity. Members of the Mithras Mysteries met in underground temples some of which still survive in large numbers to this day. The cult appears to have had its center in Rome, and was thought to be a male only association. In that tradition, Pike writes, the ascent and descent of the human soul through the seven spheres is a parallel to our symbolic journey upon the Kabbalistic Tree of Life.

It is upon this arboreal ladder, in the Judeo/Christian tradition, that Jacob in the book of Genesis is said to of witnessed heavenly angels, and the Great Architect himself, ascend and descend to and from the earth - a pattern our souls are said to undergo as we move through the stages of our spiritual existence and an interesting esoteric nod towards the Hindu tradition of reincarnation.

For perspective, we must look at several outward expressions of this climbing ascent and descent and find association in its esoteric connectivity. Cirlot, in his *Dictionary of Symbols*, goes into great length on the aspect of the ladder (more commonly attributed as stairs) which gives us an interesting Masonic association. In his work, Cirlot states very plainly the association of stars can be found through the Egyptian system of hieroglyphics by defining the act of ascent as one of the *"appellations of Osiris"* as it is he who *"stands at the top of the steps."* Osiris, the resurrected Egyptian deity, was said to be the mythological judge of the dead in the afterlife and the underworld agency that granted all life, including the flooding of the Nile and the vegetation that came from it. Interestingly, Osiris, with Isis, gave rise to the sky god Horus who is a precursor to the notion of the all-seeing eye of protection. Cirlot quotes from the Book of the Dead, which says of the purpose of the climb that *"...My steps are now in position so that I may see the gods."*[16/17] Drawing cultural references of descent and ascent upon an earthly ladder connected to the heavens represents a vehicle by which its visionary seeks communion of sorts in a *"mystical union"* with God.[18] We can see the basis of this parallel in the study of alchemy as the stages of transformation are figured as aspects upon a ladder as that is emblematic of the stages of transformation ascending and descending their states. Citing Stephan Michelspacher's work *Die Cabala, Spiegel der Kunst und Natur* (The Mirror of Art and Nature), published in 1615, the rungs of the ladder are relatable to the stages of transformation, specifically to Calcification, Sublimation, Solution, Purification, Distillation, Coagulation, and Tincture

The World and the Universe as One

IL MONTE SANTO DI DIO (THE HOLY MOUNTAIN OF GOD), 1477
ATTRIBUTED TO BACCIO BALDINI DRAWINGS BY BOTTICELLI.
PUBLISHED IN FLORENCE BY NICHOLAS OF BRESLAU,

 THE APPRENTICE

which lead to an inner shrine - a link that we can draw to the place of the outer porch of the Masonic lodge which is where the aspirant to Free Masonry is introduced to the Chamber of Reflection.

The chamber is an old aspect of Masonry that is little used in modern initiatory practice. Its purpose is to serve as a contemplative setting for the initiate to consider his existence in light of the transformation he has elected to undertake in the Masonic lodge of initiation. Within the chamber, images and symbols of life and death, time, transformation and contemplation serve as a back drop to the Latin phrase:

∴ V ∴ I ∴ T ∴ R ∴ I ∴ O ∴ L ∴

which is inscribed upon the wall in front of the aspirant. Surrounded by the symbols of a rooster, salt, sulfur, an hourglass, and a human skull, the acronym ∴ V ∴ I ∴ T ∴ R ∴ I ∴ O ∴ L ∴ is decoded to read:

VISITA INTERIORA TERRAE RECTIFICANDO INVENIES OCCULTUM LAPIDEM

Visit the interior of the earth and rectifying, you will find the hidden stone

A reference, perhaps, to the inner and outer journey in search of the mythical philosopher's stone.[19] It is in this thread that we can see the process of Ein Sof as the precursor to the activation of transformation that takes place in this degree as the chamber is the point of focus preceding entry of the neophyte into the lodgeroom.

Mircea Eliade, the Romanian historian, writer and philosopher, says that in the symbolism of the steps there is a vivid image of *"breaking through"* the levels of existence in order to open up the way from one world to another, establishing a relationship between heaven, earth, and hell.[20] We can see this idea illustrated in

THE APPRENTICE

Bettini's *Libro del Monte Santo di Dio* with a ladder as steps laid upon a mountain side showing a parallel relationship between steps and ascension. In this image, we see the aspects of elevation mingled with a process of self development as the virtues as depicted upon the rungs - aspects easily associated to the Masonic journey through the second degree.

Yet, why would Pike include such great emphasis on the ladder for it not to be included in the degree working? As a symbol, the ladder is said to be an expression of spirituality through a symbol where, as C. J. Jung explains in his work *Psychological Types*[21], the use of symbols is a means to an end - *"spirituality tries to make something spiritual out of the unconscious expression."* In this instance, the ladder becomes the representation of what the degree teaches in the expression of the ascent (and eventual descent) to that mystical connection as creator with the created and with the created to the creator. The ascent of the ladder is the journey through the stages of mental elevation which leads to a state of spiritual evolution, the gates through which we must all pass as the ancients did in the Mithraic mysteries and even older mystery schools of antiquity to pass through our stages of initiation by knowledge gained one step at a time. The metaphor that we can take from this Masonic work being that as knowledge is gained by the elevation in the blue lodge degrees we further climb in knowledge and understanding up into the Scottish Rite degrees. In this climb, we come into contact with the many *lights* of the lodge both literal and allegorical which are both specific to this first degree and to the higher degrees as we ascend into them, an ideal metaphor for constructing them upon the Tree of Life.

Reading deeply into Pike, he makes an interesting link to the Blazing Star. Said to represent *Divine Providence*, Pike dismisses the symbol as being fanciful and a modern invention.[22] Rather he draws parallel to it as a representation of knowledge and learning, the seeking of wisdom

 THE APPRENTICE

as personified through Horus of ancient Egypt, Mercury of Rome, and Hermes of Greek antiquity. Pike's attribution seems not as accidental, but as a means to link the practice of the lodge in a similar manner as that of religious institutions, whose purpose here is the reviving of the role of past Hermetic practitioners of recent antiquity so as to preserve that study within the system of the Rite. Especially as Pike describes the *"Creative energy of the deity"* which he suggests is represented as a point within the circle, reminiscent of that heliocentric idea debated centuries earlier which changed the focal point of man (on earth) as the center of the universe. It does not appear in Pike's work or in the degree that it was in the exoteric sense of man as a creator of life, but in his own physical microcosm in shaping the world within which he exists, which we became acquainted with in the world formation of the four elements (from Ein Sof to Malkuth) that the candidate is brought through in the conduct of the degree. To illustrate this point, Pike looks to the old degrees from our past Masonic working saying *"The Blazing Star of glory in the center"* which *"refers us to the grand luminary, the sun, which enlightens the earth. They called it also in the same lectures, an emblem of Prudence"* meaning *"...foresight, and accordingly, the Blazing Star has been regarded as an emblem of Omniscience, or the All Seeing Eye, which to the Egyptians initiates was an emblem of Osiris, the creative,* [and remember at top of the Egyptian Book of the Dead's ladder] *with the Yod in the center, it has the Kabbalistic meaning of the Divine Energy, manifested as light, creating the Universe."*[23] It is in that creation that the aspirant becomes the apprentice, in the formation and journey of the elements that compose his being - spiritually and physically, creating the Blazing Star.

As we have found, it would be wrong minded to suggest that Masonry is simply about the conferral of titular titles and degrees. In their evolving study, we find a wealth of knowledge

 THE APPRENTICE

that awaits discovery in each progressive step. As the apprentice takes his first tentative step in these lessons, his first task is conformity within this system - the passage from Ein Sof to Malkuth by means of an introduction to that process. Looking at the work before us, we find that it is indeed a complex lesson of the esoteric systems of initiation influenced by the Judaic study of the Kabbalah, but woven into a tapestry of tradition that shares, if not cogent links, metaphorical connections to the ancient mystery traditions of Rome and Egypt. At their lowest common denominator, together they create an initiation into a symbolic system forming a bond by means of shared experience, a small act with a larger parallel, or better said as creating *order out of chaos*. Following our own path into the degree, we become the substance transformed as earth, water, fire, and spirit while taken upon our trials that leads us to the allegorical ladder, crowned by Osiris, the Blazing Star of wisdom through knowledge, representing our climb into the system of the Rite. Certainly, it could be made more arbitrary with significant change applied, but Pike devised a plan to link the Rite in its reorganization to the traditions of mystical Christianity and alchemy that flourished in the underground cabals across Europe just a few short centuries before the time of his writing. His design, it seems, was not to recreate the study of Jewish mysticism, but to build upon it by applying attributes of Christian mysticism and reorganizing it so as to capture the best of its predecessor's faith and finding its parallels with its more ancient traditions of knowledge and wisdom. Pike undoubtedly made the invention to link the process, a link it seems that most practitioners fail to fully appreciate, to disregard the dogmatic constrictions of faith and religious eschatology for the broader parallels and nuance of what that faith means - its potential rather than its apocalypse. In approaching the degree and underscoring its transformation, the aspirant of the First Degree enters onto the Tree of

 THE APPRENTICE

Life and becomes a student of its teachings as Pike sees it, quite literally being brought from the chaos of Ein Sof to the elemental perfection that is in the structure of Malkuth. It is through this first degree of Scottish Rite masonry that we begin our instruction in that Hermetic Philosophy of man as the creative energy of creation outside of the cosmic framework of dogmatic religious practice. The parallel to which is that of man made in God's image - Adam, god on Earth, as the terrestrial creative energy of creation - Ein Sof made manifest as Malkuth. Pike announces this in his connecting man to the Blazing Star when he says that every student of this system is to be *"true, [philosophically] and seek to find and learn the Truth, [these] are the great objects of every good Mason."* These words of Pike's, at the closing of his commentary, illuminate the purpose of our quest which is to seek truth, in whatever form it takes, which comes from our spiritual quest of knowledge. One can only add that it is our obligation as a Mason or one who holds these principals of truth, to follow this path for both our own being and for the broader well-being of humanity. That the true object of mankind is that *Blazing Star of Knowledge* given to us as we traverse upon the ladder between the heavens and the earth. Perhaps Kircher had it right that the Sephirot of Malkuth, is an *Assisting Intelligence* giving us the impetus to find a sense of direction through our process of elemental change. Our conduit to the degrees is the ladder we climb which conveys us up and into the endeavor before us in the *Great Work* and within the Scottish Rite. In doing our work, we begin our travels up and down its steps from the mundane *Prima Materia* to the sacred celestial apartments in the many branches that will construct our search for further light upon the Tree of Life.

SPIRITUAL INITIATION

The process of initiation begins with death. Not the universal conception of physical expiration, the fate of which we forever move towards, rather this death is the transformation of ideas, in so much as we may understand them which will invariably lead to a different transcendental state of being. As we think of death in a negative light, perhaps a better way to understand it is as a metamorphosis, like a caterpillar cocooning itself so as to be transformed into a majestic butterfly to continue on its existence. Such is this preliminary stage of initiation such as we have in the Rites of Freemasonry.

Yet, these rites are not a singularly unique attribute to the storied fraternity. Initiation occurs

 THE APPRENTICE

at all levels of society in all corners of life. We see this in the rites of baptism of faith, the oaths of association, or the undertaking of a task of consequence. What these paths illustrate are various stages of life initiations and denotations as marking points of significant change in the individual who undertakes them. The death of the old with the birth of the new. To use a more colorful metaphor, these are our journeys up and down upon the heaven-bound ladder from Jacob's dream in Genesis, a journey which occurs many times in our lives to higher plateaus and to lower levels of our being. At each stage of attainment, we undergo another initiation in developing our true selves, while leaving behind the dead hush of what was before.

In making the study of the first degree, the notion that stood firmest in its consideration is that *from chaos comes order*, and from over that threshold, we leave our prior selves so as to become a new being. Such is the idea behind the movement from the chaotic Ain Sof into the

Kabbalistic Sephirot of Malkuth.

It is in that passage from chaos that we transform from that wild unrestrained force that Pike wrote about into that pinpoint focus of light composed of the four elements of matter which in turn compose the entirety of the universe. This is not intended to represent a theological argument of creation, rather as a means to put into context our existence as the stuff composed of material from the stars. We are below as the universe is above just as the universe above is so composed of what is below. This insight makes for an interesting consideration towards the point within the circle.

Symbolically unique to Freemasonry, the symbol has a wider subtext as the element of air, one of the four key alchemical elements of antiquity. Without delving to deeply into its broader considerations, most representations of the compass circumscribed point depict it as a flat, two-dimensional, shape without greater form. Using an older consideration, the point

within the circle once depicted the Egyptian creator god Ra, who was the raw creative power symbolized in the mid-day sun. So then, in syncretic fashion, as those who undertake the path of initiation, too, become like Ra and assume the mantle of creator. We, the stuff of stars, assume in parallel the role of the universe here in and around in our ongoing existence - a notion that coalesces into the idea that *the world as the universe is as one*. Not only are we of the universe, but so too are we a part of it, the single point of creative light at its center - the point within our circle.

For those who need see this in a tarotic correspondence, the initiation undertaken from the chaos of Ain Sof into the sphere of Malkuth is represented in the card of the four 10's, where heaven and earth are balanced between the four elements. From the elements come the wonderful existence of our creative heaven on earth, an application of our existence above as below, establishing for ourselves a *Prima Materia* in

SPIRITUAL INITIATION

Malkuth from which to ascend higher into the celestial apartments of the divine.

Such is the journey and path of the apprentice, the figurative soul, who undergoes a metaphorical death so as to undergo a spiritual initiation - the transportation from the mundane to the celestial, which is our entry point onto the allegorical Tree of Life. This journey begins with passing through a state of transformation leaving behind the raw primal state of change and chaos to enter upon a path of seeking the divine. We all, like the hermetic initiate, desire to see and know all that there is to be understood, and it is in this pattern of initiation that our lessons begin to unfold their wisdoms to us. This is our climbing ascent upon the ladder and the initiation we seek.

So in death we assume life as we move from our state of chaos below to our comportment above, ever moving from state to state and undertaking new lessons and initiations so as to become apprentices to attain the role of mas-

ter within the lessons of the *Great Work*. The metaphorical death is where our journey ends and where our process of realizing our potential possibilities begins. From chaos comes order so as to see our role in the heaven of our creation which is here upon earth and the divine natures above us.

ORDER FROM CHAOS

Upon the frontispiece of this short work is an illustration depicting the transformative journey from chaos to order - from Ain Sof into the sphere of Malkuth.

Those looking upon this image for the conventions of Masonic initiation will not see them and become quickly lost in its relevant symbolism and devices. While this board purports to hold secret symbolism, its allegorical lesson is not in its many parts, but in its overall message of transformation. What it represents is initiation and transformation, from chaos to order, presenting the initiate the opportunity to ascend higher into the limbs of the majestic Kabbalistic Tree of Life, itself a metaphor of transformation

THE APPRENTICE

in understanding our evolution to the divine.

The chaos from which we come is like a convolution of roots warped and entwined, choking and starving for nourishment that comes from the light above. Its network striking deep into the foundations of the *Prima Materia*, the primal earth, never knowing or understanding that their nourishment and growth comes from above.

Out of this choking chaos, rising as if from a primordial soup, the apprentice initiate coalesces by giving birth to new thought and inspiration. To attain this place, the initiate must first traverse the threshold of the checkered pavement and tessellated edge so as to assume his figurative state of perfection as a human manifestation of the creative universe - man and the universe as one.

Framing this cosmic correlation are the four worlds: the land upon which he walks, the firmament above adorning the land with its nourishing rains and cooling clouds, and the star decked canopy from which our terrestrial essence of the four elements was created and delivered to our mote of life upon the celestial winds of the universe's creation.

This is the manifestation of the Sephirot of Malkuth, our beginning journey upon the Tree of Life and the esoteric convention of our spiritual unfolding. Borrowing from another idea of spiritual unfolding, out of the center of this work is a universe wheel - the point within the circle - the dimensional representation of the universe that enfolds us as we sit within its center. But so too is it a representation of ourselves as we unfold the universe around us, an idea which speaks through the words - *the world as the universe as one* or the Hermetic axiom *as above so below, as below so to as above*. This is the Helios of creation, the nexus of creative power which can only come from order made out of chaos. The rings of this point within the circle serve to represent more a sphere than a flat, two-dimensional depiction and serve to suggest

the four elements of creation which go into its creation. These elements, described from the classic alchemist's conception of transformation include earth, air, fire, and water which, together, in their myriad combinations serve to represent the whole of our universe and the creation within it. From that point at the center rise three paths though not independent of one another.

The ladder is indicative of Jacob's dream upon which angels are seen to ascend and descend from heaven to earth and back again. Here the ladder takes on a new representation of ascent from a place as its use is suggestive of moving upon the several paths rather than as a solitary otherworldly conveyance to heaven. No, in fact, the ladder is merely a manifestation of things to come as little in this symbolic landscape ever remains the same or holds to its singular meaning.

On the left of the ladder is a representation of entropy and time, in the snake of eternity. As students of the Western Esoteric tradition will know, the tree of life grows and branches from

Malkuth, but here we get only a glimpse of the path of severity and mercy. For now we are firmly in the hand of wisdom from where we begin our manifestation of study. The snake is not intended as a threat, but rather as a reminder of time and reflection that no one is beyond the shadow of eternity and all we do that is worthy of memory must need be done here and now while upon this earth.

By contrast, the owl upon the right path is a lesson in understanding that from wisdom comes understanding. This ancient symbol of knowledge is a passage of knowing ourselves so that to our own selves, can we be true. It stands as a reminder not in the path of wisdom, but in the path of understanding so as to point the way of our enfoldment, encouraging us to climb ever higher in our pursuit of knowledge.

At its sum, this image of Ain Sof into Malkuth is the journey of the craftsman through his stage as an apprentice entering into the *Great Work* and the development of his higher self - be

it a Masonic system or another symbolic tradition of Hermetic study from which initiation is the beginning. This is the first glimpse of the great journey, the gate through which we travel into the deeper recesses of the unknown and our higher selves.

So Mote it Be

NOTES

Ein Sof

From the Jewish Encyclopedia (1906), the *Zohar* explains the term Ein Sof as: *"Before He gave any shape to the world, before He produced any form, He was alone, without form and without resemblance to anything else. Who then can comprehend how He was before the Creation? Hence it is forbidden to lend Him any form or similitude, or even to call Him by His sacred name, or to indicate Him by a single letter or a single point... But after He created the form of the Heavenly Man, He used him as a chariot wherein to descend, and He wishes to be called after His form, which is the sacred name "YHWH". "Ein Sof" signifies "the nameless being."*

In another passage the Zohar reduces the term to

THE APPRENTICE

"Ein" (non-existent), because God so transcends human understanding as to be practically non-existent. The limitless notion of the divine."

In addition to the Sefer Yetzirah and the Zohar, other well-known explications of the relation between Ein Sof and all other realities and levels of reality have been formulated by the Jewish mystical thinkers of the Middle Ages, such as Isaac the Blind and Azriel. Judah HayyaT, in his commentary MinHat Yehudah on the Ma'areket Elahut, gives the following explanation of the term "Ein Sof":

"Any name of God which is found in the Bible can not be applied to the Deity prior to His self-manifestation in the Creation, because the letters of those names were produced only after the emanation. . . . Moreover, a name implies a limitation in its bearer; and this is impossible in connection with the 'Ein Sof.'"

Sephirot

The term denotes the ten major junctions within the Kabbalastic Tree of Life, typically illustrated as spheres which are the conjunctive points within it's understanding. The 10 Sephirot are connected by 22 paths which facilitate a transportation of sorts through the various Sephirot rendering their own lessons, allegories and symbols.

Malkuth

Malkuth, or Shekhinah, is the tenth Sephirot in the Kabbalistic configuration of Tree of Life. Found at the bottom of the Tree. It's placement is upon the middle pillar of Wisdom. In the traditional sense, this sephirah is the furthest from the spiritual emination of the divine source and the last stage of progression in its esoteric study.

Unlike the other Sephirot, Malkuth is an attribute of God that does not emanate from God directly. Rather it comes from the divines creation - when that creation reflects the deities radient glory from within itself.

Malkuth is said to represent the Kingdom and is associated with the realm of the earth

 THE APPRENTICE

(or matter) relating to the physical world - the *Prima Materia*. While the 10th Sephirot in the Judaic Kabbalah, in the Scottish Rite configuration it is the first and the entry point of the candidate into the degree from the chaos of the limitless divine source of the Ain Sof.

Allegorically, Malkuth is composed of the tangible elements of earth, fire and water and bound together with spirit (air) which gives life to the sphere.

FOOTNOTES

1. No known catalog of ritual practice comparisons is believed to exist.

2. Such traditions are likely, in the opinion of the author, outgrowths and parallel developments of the work of Pike in *Morals and Dogma* and the Scottish Rite. Such groups include the Golden Dawn, Ordo Templi Orientis, Thelema, Builders of the Adytum, Theosophy, and other simillar Hermetic systems.

3. Kaplan, Aryeh. *Sefer Yetzirah: the book of creation*. York Beach, Maine: Weiser, 1990. Print.

4. From the S*epher Yezirah*, Chapter 1 - Section 1: Yah, the Lord of hosts, the living God, King of the Universe, Omnipotent, All-Kind and Merciful, Supreme and Extolled, who is Eternal, Sublime and Most-Holy, ordained (formed) and created the Universe in thirty-two mysterious paths of wisdom by

THE APPRENTICE

three Sepharim, namely: 1) S'for ספר

2) Sippur ספור

3) Sapher זרפסו which are in Him one and the same. They consist of a decade out of nothing and of twenty-two fundamental letters. He divided the twenty-two consonants into three divisions:

1) three אמות mothers, fundamental letters or first elements
2) seven double
3) twelve simple consonants.

Retrieved from Sacred-Texts at http://www.sacred-texts.com/jud/sy/sy02.htm

5. *Bibliographie Giovanni Pico della Mirandola.* Bienvenue aux éditions de l'éclat. N.p., n.d. Web. 17 June 2011 http://www.lyber-eclat.net/lyber/mirandola/picbio.html

6. As attributed to Aristotle, a *Primal Chaos*, said to be the foundation of reality, though the connection to Aristotle has some contention. We can look to Ovid (1st century BC), in his *Metamorphoses*, who described Chaos as "a rude and undeveloped mass, that nothing made except a ponderous weight; and all discordant elements confused, were there congested in a shapeless heap." which may give a better understanding.

FOOTNOTES

7. Szulakowska, Urszula. *The alchemy of light: geometry and optics in late Renaissance alchemical illustration.* Leiden: Brill, 2000. Print. p. 92 - *Von hylealischen das ist, pri-materialischen catholischen, oder algemeinemx natürlichen ... chaos der naturgemässen alchymiae und alchymisten, wiederholete, verneuerte und wolvermehrete naturgemäss-alchymisch- und rechtlehrende philosophische Confessio oder Bekandtniss ... Deme beygefügt ist eine treuhertzige Wahrnungs-Vermahnung an alle wahre Alchymisten, sich vor den betrügerischen Arg-Chymisten zu hüten.* Magdeburg. 1597.

Roughly translated: *From hylealischen that is , pri - materia metallic catholischen , or algemeinemx natural ... chaos of nature according alchymiae and alchemists , wiederholete , verneuerte and wolvermehrete naturally - alchymisch- and right -teaching philosophical Confessio or Bekandtniss ... Deme is prefixed, a treuhertzige True -drying exhortation to all true alchemists , to beware of fraudulent Arg - chymists*

8. Regardie, Israel; Cicero, Chic and Sandra. *A Garden of Pomegranates: Skrying on the Tree of Life.* 3rd ed., ed. St. Paul, Minn. Llewellyn Pub, 1999. Print. p. 55

9. *Oedipus Aegyptiacus* – Athanasius Kircher

 THE APPRENTICE

10. A∴A∴ is the Argenteum Astrum from the skygodproject.net website - now offline, from printed edition.

11. Ritual working under the Grand Lodge of Louisiana ritual, revised 1963

12. Fortune, Dion. *The Mystical Qabalah* . Rev. ed. York Beach, ME: Samuel Weiser, 2000. Print.

13. Louisiana degree workings - the instruction of the W.M. on the first journey of the candidate, the journey of fire.

14. Tester, S. J.. *A History of Western Astrology*. Woodbridge, Suffolk: Boydell Press, 1987. Print. p.104

15. Clauss, Manfred. *The Roman Cult of Mithras: the god and his mysteries*. Edinburgh: Edinburgh University Press, 2000. Print. p.102

16. Budge, Ernest Alfred Tompson Wallis. *The Book of the Dead, an English translation of the chapters, hymns, etc., of the Theban recension*. Falmouth, Massaschusets: Harvard University, 1901. Print.

17. Cirlot, Juan Eduardo. *A Dictionary of Symbols* . New York:

FOOTNOTES

Philosophical Library, 1962. Print.p. 312

18. Ibid

19. The philosophers' stone is that legendary alchemical substance believed to be capable of transmuting base metal into gold. It is also suggested, in antiquity, to be an elixir of life, used for rejuvenation and immortality. In time, the notion of the philosophers' stone became the central symbol of mystical alchemy, the term coming to symbolize perfection at its finest, true enlightenment and a sort of heavenly bliss that comes with understanding the divine aspect of deity. The work towards discovering the philosophers' stone became known as the *Great Work* often written in Latin as a *Magnum Opus*.

20. Cirlot citing Eliade, Mircea. *Mephistopheles and the Androgyne; studies in religious myth and symbol*. New York: Sheed and Ward, 1965. Print. Cirlot p. 313

21. *Psychological Types,* N.Y. Harcourt, Brace and Company, 1933. Print. p. 609

22. Pike, Albert, *Morals and Dogma* p. 15

23. Ibid

INDEX

A

Adam 54, 55, 74
Ain Sof 78, 80, 83
air 47, 59, 79
alchemy 48, 58, 64, 79
   alchemical process 59
allegorical 83
All Seeing Eye 71
ancient mysteries 58
angelic evocation 40
apprentice 81
Apprentice 59
Argenteum Astrum 52
Assisting Intelligence 52, 75
astrology 44, 60

B

baptism 78
being 78
Blazing Star 69, 71, 72, 74
Book of the Dead 64, 71

C

Cabala 39, 42, 44
Calcification 64
Chamber of Reflection 66
chaos 46, 54, 78, 79, 80, 81, 82, 83, 84, 85
Chaos 48, 58
chaotic 48
chaotic state 55
checkered floor 56
checkered pavement 84
Christian Cabalah 45
Christian Mysticism 39
Cirlot 63, 64
Coagulation 66
consciousness 46
Corpus Hermeticium 44
Creation XXVI

D

death 77, 81, 82
Dictionary of Symbols 63
Distillation 66
Divine Energy 71

divine natures 82
Divine Providence 69

E

earth 47, 57, 58, 72
Ein Sof XXXIV, 41, 47, 48, 49, 50, 67, 70, 72
EIN SOF XXIV
elemental trials 59
elements 58
elements, four 54, 70, 85
Eliade, Mircea 67
Enocian 44
Entered Apprentice 56

F

fire 47, 57, 58, 72
First Degree 55
force 49
Fortune, Dion 55
Freemasonry XV, XVI, 39, 42, 43, 77

G

Gate 56, 57
Genesis 54, 55, 63, 78
Gnosticism 44
God 48, 49, 55, 64, 65
Golden Dawn 48, 52, 53
Great Architect 55, 63
Great Work 82, 87
gunpowder 50

H

Hermes Trismegistus 44
  Hermes 70
Hermetic 39, 43, 44, 70, 85
  Hermetic Philosophy 74
hermetic initiate 81
Hermeticism 44
Hermetic Qabalah 45
Hermetic study 88
Hermetism 44
higher selves 88
Horus 64, 69

I

initiation 66, 72, 83

J

Jacob's ladder 60
  Jacob's dream 78
John the Baptist 59
Judaism 38, 43
  Jewish mysticism 73
Jung, C. J. 68

K

Kabbalah 37, 38, 39, 40, 41, 42, 43, 44, 48, 53, 55, 72
  Qabalah 39
Kether 50
Khunrath, Heinrich 48

Kircher 52, 53, 75

L

ladder 81
light 54, 57

M

magical practice 40
Malkuth 41, 47, 49, 50, 52, 55, 56, 70, 72, 74, 75, 79, 80, 81, 83, 85
Medici 44
Mercury 70
metamorphosis 77
Michelspacher, Stephan 64
Mirandola, Pico della 43
Mithraic Mystery traditions 60
  Mithras mysteries 69
  Sol 62
Mithras 60, 62
Morals and Dogma XIII, 37, 45, 49, 60
Mystery School Qabalah 50
mystical Christianity 73
Mystical Qabalah, The 55
mystical traditions 47

N

neo-paganism 45
Neo-Platonism 44
New Age 44

O

oaths 78
Oedipus Aegyptiacus 52
order 78, 83, 85
order out of the chaos 47
Osiris 63, 64, 71, 72

P

Paracelsus 48
paths 37
philosopher's stone 67
Phoenix 58
Pike, Albert 36, 39, 40, 49, 50, 60, 68, 79
point within the circle 70, 79, 80, 85
Prima Materia 47, 48, 75, 80, 84
primeval chaos 48
Prudence 71
Psychological Types 68
Purification 64

Q

Quatuor Coronati Lodge XVIII

R

Ra 80
Rabbinic Judaism 42
Regardie, Israel 48, 56

religious practice 39
Roman 43
Rosicrucianism 44

S

Scottish Rite XVI, XVIII, 36, 37, 40, 42, 50, 53, 59, 69, 74
self 41, 59
Sepher Yetzirah 42
Sephirot 37, 41, 55, 56, 85
Sephiroth 47
Shekhinah 48
Solomnic angelic magick 44
Solution 64
spirit 59, 72
spiritual elements 47
Sublimation 64
Suda 60
symbols 66

T

tarot 80
Tarot 44
tessellated 56, 84
Tincture 66

transformation 77
Tree of Life 37, 40, 41, 42, 45, 51, 62, 69, 73, 75, 81, 83
Truth 74

U

universe 55

V

V.I.T.R.I.O.L. 66

W

water 47, 57, 58, 72
Western esoteric system 50
wisdom 72

Y

Yod 71
York Rite 35, 36, 59

Z

Zohar 48

www.ingramcontent.com/pod-product-compliance
Lightning Source LLC
Chambersburg PA
CBHW070818100426
42813CB00033B/3427/J